How To Become A Successful Young Man

Diamond D. McNulty

Dedication

This book is dedicated to my mother, Londa Gray, who taught me persistence, hard work, and dedication. She devoted her life to making sure her children had everything even if she had nothing. Her daily motivation and unconditional love drove me to finish everything I set out to accomplish. She was the first one who told me, "It's Possible." Thank you, Mom, for believing in me and pushing me to be a leader in life.

I would also like to dedicate this book to my lifetime teacher and mentor, Mr. Abdul Muhammad. Ever since I entered your classroom at the age of sixteen you have always given me great knowledge and advice to accomplish my dreams. You have opened my eyes to things that I hadn't experienced before, which gave me a head start to become a force in this society. Words can't explain your honor. Thank you for every book suggestion, life connection and perseverance speech you ever gave me. Because I listened to you, I am now on the path to succeed and reach my dreams.

Thank you.

TABLE OF CONTENTS

ACKNOWLEDGMENTS

I would like to thank my family and friends for supporting me throughout my lifetime in this fight to "take over the world". I want you and everyone else in the world to know that you can become anything you want to become. It all starts with your plan.

I would also like to thank every individual reading this book looking to gain the knowledge and mindset it really takes to become successful in life. I love you. If no one has ever told you that they love you, I do! I love every adult that has come before me and every child who will come after me. I believe success is truly the only goal we all should reach for in life, and with that my main goal is to "Make A Difference".

I might have to change my name to Bill Buffett (Bill Gates and Warren Buffett) in my later years because that's how much of an impact I plan to make in the world. Just kidding about the names but seriously you have to feel the greatness within you and use that as fuel to accomplish your goals. Remember I love you and I wish you well on your journey toward success.

Special Thanks

I want to give a special thanks to Michele Brown, Denisha Bryant and Steve Brett for reading my book before its release and giving me great feedback, which was truly valuable in making this a phenomenal book. I would also like to thank Carrie J. Coleman for helping me finish this process in a strong fashion. In life we all know it's not how you start but how you finish. Thank you all!

How this book came about...

One day, I was at home relaxing after working doubles all week and my younger brother Dominic came over to visit me. He started asking me all these questions about success and how I overcame certain things. It made me feel really good because, since I had been through so much in life, I was able to give him knowledge on so many topics.

While I was talking to him, in mid-sentence I stopped and said, "Bro, you know what... I'm sure there are a lot of young men out there who need to know everything that I'm telling you right now. I'm going to write a book!" A few years later... Here we are!

PREFACE

"If you fail to plan, you plan to fail."
- Benjamin Franklin

LOOK AROUND YOU!

How many young men your age are reading this
book? Not many. You have already taken the first
step to success.

Once you are 16 years old or older, you
have to understand that you are no
longer a kid and you should be
thinking seriously about what you want to be in life.
If you missed what I said, here is the previous line
once more…**"Once you turn 16 years old, you
have to understand that you are no longer a kid
and you should be thinking seriously about what
you want to be in life."** This is when you come up

with your success plan.

At the age of 16, you are at the beginning stages of manhood. This point is critical because you have to develop your mind into thinking like an adult while still being looked at as a child. The decisions you make from this moment forward will show how responsible or irresponsible you are. Your reputation for being responsible begins now, and, believe me, being responsible is very important.

In this book I plan to teach you some fundamental principles that will open doors for you once you begin to master them. So follow along as we take the journey to becoming a successful young man. Focus… It's time to take over the world. Let's go!

CHAPTER 1

When I Grow Up

When thinking about your life and growing up,

you should ask yourself 3 questions.

When answering these 3 questions I want you to

be bold and reach for the stars! Don't limit your

dreams to what you think is possible, write down

those things that you think are impossible and

then make it a goal to achieve those very things.

Make Them Possible!

First Question:

What do you want to be in life?

Doctor, lawyer, political figure, entrepreneur, sports

owner, etc...

(For notes, use the Note Section at the end of each chapter.)

If you want to become more than one thing, I suggest you strategically create a plan that will lead you to success. But for now, think of that one thing you like to do that you enjoy the most.

Ok, you got it? Now align your plans and life journey with that one thing that you enjoy doing the most. Then, if you want to incorporate your other interests, create as many connecting pathways as you want along that same journey roadmap.

Example - When I was younger, I said I wanted to become a chef, but I also loved to take pictures. So I wanted to become a chef and a photographer. Consequently, I chose culinary arts as my career path (what I enjoyed the most) and photography as my hobby (my other interest) until I was able to bring in enough money from photography to make photography another sustaining career (the connecting pathway I created). Now I have a catering company and a photography company (plan executed).

<u>Second Question</u>:

What is everything you want to accomplish/or acquire in life?

Win awards, buy a house, car, spouse, kids, travel, become a role model, etc.

This question can have unlimited answers but focus on the major accomplishments you would like to achieve in life first. As you answer the question consider the following: How will you better your life and the lives of those around you? Working hard and/or being a positive role model? How will you make a difference in society? Give back to the youth, become a volunteer, a mentor or a philanthropist?

What steps do you need to take to achieve your goals?

The steps you need to achieve your goals and dreams require (4) things:

1. Research

2. Asking Questions

3. Planning

4. Decision Making

Research. After you decide what you want to be in life, you have to be proactive and research what it takes to become that which you choose. In doing your research (i.e. online or library), you can find out the best schools for your field, top employers hiring for that field, and the amount of money you can make in your field of choice. After you do your research, you will now understand what it will take to become whatever you have just chosen and if it fits your vision of what you want to achieve.

Ask Questions. If you decide that you are still interested in that career at that point, find someone in that field who you look up to and ask them a few questions regarding that profession. Get some insight on the pros and cons in making that career choice. **Note** - Only ask people who are knowledgeable about the career choice you are choosing because you never want to take advice from individuals who are not informed on the subject.

Plan. Start to look deep into how you are going to get from where you are to where you want to be in life. Every plan that I have ever created started from within. I would sit in a quiet room, analyze my current situation and ask myself questions.

For Example (My Roadmap):

How will I become an executive chef?

- Graduate high school (Good grades)
- Get a scholarship, loan or have my parents help pay for college
- Go to culinary school
- Get a job in a restaurant, hotel or kitchen
- Learn and develop my skills
- Transfer between companies and meet new people

- Gain credibility and go through the ranks of promotion from sous chef to tournant chef to executive sous chef, until I become an executive chef.

In order to grasp anything in life you have to see it in your mind first and get a clear view of exactly what you want.

Decision Making. Once you decide that you have seen enough and you feel confident that you can accomplish your dreams by putting in the necessary work, draw out a roadmap (vision board) of plans from start to finish. This plan should illustrate how you will get from where you are now to where you want to be in the future. Once your decisions are made and you are all in—stick to the plan!

Short Story

At the age of 19, I started noticing that I was mentally outgrowing my environment. You have to understand that where you are doesn't define where you are going. Your past or present doesn't define your future. I remember that realization like it was yesterday. I was parked in the back of the Cabrini Green project building with some friends when about 5 police cars surrounded my car. They stated that they got a call that we had guns out there.

I just laughed it off because I knew we were clean. More importantly, I understood the perception of what they were thinking ... young black males in a bad neighborhood with a nice car. My instinct started to kick in and at that very moment I knew it was time for a change.

Every other day after that, I kept getting pulled over in the same areas. It was as if they were trying to gain more information on who I was and how I attained what I had because I looked very young and was driving a brand new car. The kicker was that everything I had was legal because I was working as a chef at a hotel that was paying me fairly well at 19 years old.

Around this time a lot of negative things started to go on around me, and I was becoming overwhelmed with what I knew eventually could soon end up bad. In the heat of the moment, I planned a trip to visit my sister in Louisiana for a vacation that she wanted me to take a long time ago. That vacation changed my life.

In Louisiana it was so peaceful and welcoming that I wanted to stay. My sister said, "Hey D' , if you move down here you're going to be rich, especially how you think."

I said, "You know what, you're right, Sis, I will move down here."

I talked to my brother down there who already had his own apartment and he said, "Sure."

I went back home, put in my two weeks' notice at work, kissed my mother and told her, "I have to go."

I left for Louisiana with $200 in my pocket, credit card debt and a $380 car note. That was a turning point in my life! <u>Sometimes you have to make key decisions that will remove you from negative environments and/or people in order to have a chance to develop into a better you.</u> When I left Chicago, I was in debt and I knew I would have to work 3 times as hard to bounce back, but I made the decision to do it. That key decision is the reason I am so successful today.

There will be key moments in your life where you have to make life-changing decisions! Don't be scared to step out on faith. – Diamond McNulty

NOTES

CHAPTER 1 REVIEW

What are the (3) questions you should ask yourself when thinking about life?

What are the 4 steps you need to take to achieve your goals?

What is the name of the board you will create as your roadmap to success?

There will be _____ moments in your life where you have to make life-changing decisions.

Never be afraid to step out on _____.

CHAPTER 2

Bro's, Boyz And Your Crew

Friendship is very important in your journey toward success. Right now, you want to analyze your friends by asking them about their plans to become successful so that you can determine whether to keep those friends close or open your circle to finding new ones with similar views to yours.

Friends come in different categories, for example:

(1) Entertainment-Oriented Friends

- The Jokester

- The Relaxed and Amusing

(2) Business-Oriented Friends

15

- Focused

- Crafty and/or Serious Natured

For instance, you have the entertainment-oriented friends who are great when it's time to party, relax and take your mind off work. But you don't want to get too distracted by the lack of focus some of these friends carry and lose sight of your plans and goals. Then you have the business-oriented friends who are great when you are looking for personal development and ways to grow and improve toward success in life.

Each category of friends has their pros and cons. You might have some friends who you trust with your secrets, like to party and hang out with, but, on a business level, they don't care to talk about future goals and plans. Not everyone will have goals and dreams, but, no matter what you do, don't let anyone talk you out of yours. If you find yourself around dream killers, get rid of them. If you have friends who are well-rounded in both categories, that's great, but if not, your circle of friends should include a mixture of both business-oriented and entertainment-oriented friends in order to keep you focused and grounded.

Stay positive, stay focused and stay surrounded by motivated people who are headed in the same direction you are.

DON'T BURN BRIDGES

What is burning bridges? Burning bridges refers to all of the good relationships you have, whether they are business relationships or personal relationships that end on a bad note. By burning that bridge, you are likely getting rid of a good relationship that you may need in the future. You could try to fix the relationship, but more than likely there is little you can do to get it back to the way it was once the damage is done.

Allowing your attitude/temper to get the best of you by making senseless decisions could damage other ventures (goals) in life that you are trying to pursue.

Everyone you have had a bad encounter with could have a negative opinion of you when speaking to others. This could reflect badly when it comes to others helping you in the future, so maintain positive relationships. Remember, word of mouth is the most powerful way of marketing, whether it's through people or products. Learning to deal with negative situations in a positive way gives you the advantage.

When faced with negativity, remember to stay calm and pay attention because there is always something to learn. You may need to distance yourself from someone or from a place where things are not going well. Basically, you want to get out of the situation without leaving a bad image of yourself (always try to be the bigger person).

Sometimes people will burn bridges with you, and you will have to decide whether they are worthy of having a relationship with you. Try to distance yourself from any drama and remember the word value. Is this relationship of any value to you? Think about it; can you benefit from having a relationship with this person? How much do you value this relationship? How much do they value you?

YOUR FUTURE CIRCLE

Your circle will change as you grow older and progress in life. This circle should consist of a few key people: your spouse, your circles of trustees (who are all the friends over the years you can look up to for guidance and call for answers), a banker, a lawyer, an accountant and other people who can assist in helping you grow personally, i.e. mentors.

Not only are they able to help you, but you should be able to help them as well. Go to the bookstore, grab a couple of books and read about what their jobs entails because you have to know how to utilize these individuals to the greatest extent. Build your team!

It took me a long time to learn everyone in my circle. I invested a lot of time and money in helping others who didn't help themselves or me. It took me a long time to realize my true value and to surround myself with people like me who focus on success. In order to get to the next level in life you have to trust yourself and others.

You have to be able to make tough decisions and let go of the people who will hold you back. Surround yourself with dreamers. Keep in mind that some people are assets and others are liabilities. Learning the true definition of assets and liabilities will make you more aware of what's really important, not only with people but in life.

Short Story

Growing up I had many friends. I had friends who sold drugs, I had friends who were sports stars and I had friends who were lames—who weren't popular at all. I was the kind of kid who could blend into any crowd because I was a great baseball player, which led me to become popular enough to be respected by the popular and low key enough to hang with some unpopular people. I watched some of my drug-dealing friends run from the police and get slapped around by older gang members. Also I watched some of my sport star friends excel, some get distracted by girls and others have babies.

Having my eyes and ears open to the streets, I had to pay attention and strategically pick up the good and leave the bad. I knew right from wrong so I did my best to make smart decisions, which is why I never joined a gang. Plus I didn't want to limit my circle of friends.

I didn't sell drugs even though the money was tempting and I was only receiving $113 a month from child support. I decided to wait until I was old enough to get a job instead of taking the risk of selling drugs. One day, I was outside with some friends and one of them pulled out a full bankroll of money and asked me did I need anything and I said, "No, I'm good, bro." I didn't say no because I didn't need the money, I said no because I never liked people to hold what they did for me over my head, like I owed them something. (Note: Be cautious when taking money from certain individuals.) Once people think you owe them they will expect you to do things against your own will to pay your debt off.

"Don't try to be different, just be good. To be good is to be different enough". – Arthur Freed

<u>NOTES</u>

CHAPTER 2 REVIEW

Name the two types of friends you will have in life.

Define Burning Bridges.

Define Assets.

Define Liabilities.

CHAPTER 3

Make The Choice

DESTROY BAD HABITS

When it comes to having a habit, I want you to

remember three things…

Habits Cost! Habits Cost! Habits Cost!

Not only do habits cost, but bad habits like smoking or excessive drinking and drugs can lead to major health problems. I never was a smoker because if I added up the amount that I would spend on cigarettes or other smoking items, (i.e. weed) it is a ridiculous amount of money. Now, if you can take all that money and put it in the bank or invest it into a business, you will benefit more.

Have fun in life but, whatever you decide to do, remember there are always consequences for your actions. Some people love to eat; some people love to party; some people love to travel or go to concerts... Limit yourself according to your lifestyle (income vs. expenses).

STAY OUT OF TROUBLE

Staying out of trouble is not hard to do unless you spend all your free time doing nothing. Fill all of your empty time with projects, whether you're cleaning the house, organizing your ideas, creating logos, reading a book or anything you care to do.

Remember one wrong decision can be life changing and may cause you to be sent to jail or cost you your life. Surround yourself with positive people

from the beginning and let everything negative fade
off.

WAIT TO HAVE KIDS

In today's society, more kids are having kids. I
can honestly say it's hard for me, at the age of 25,
with 2 jobs, living on my own, taking care of bills,
budgeting and balancing the everyday situations that
occur to even consider a baby. I can only imagine all
the things I would have to sacrifice in order to take
care of a child.

Take your time, and don't have kids until you get
married. If you can manage to beat the odds, you
will thank me because feelings change as you grow
and people change as they grow. You don't want to
jeopardize your future by being reckless and possibly
becoming dependent on your parents to raise you

and your children. Life is about balance, making smart decisions and protecting yourself.

There are 5 reasons why I would suggest you don't have any kids at an early age:

1. Live Out Your Youth

2. Finish School – Build A Career

3. Travel

4. Find The Right Person

5. Build Your Finances

Live Out Your Youth. As a child, you don't have many responsibilities and you depend on your parents or guardians for some sort of protection whether it's food, shelter or clothing. As you get older and more mature, you will start to make better decisions and support yourself and your own children if need be. By having children at a young age, you could slow your own development and stagger your mental growth due to the sudden responsibilities of parenthood. Never limit yourself, your lifestyle or a child's lifestyle due to bad decisions.

Finish School – Build A Career. Finishing school and starting a career before you have children is great. Not only will you have more time on your hands, you will be in a position to support your family financially because you are finished with school and into your career earning a living.

Travel. How many vacations have you been on so far? You can travel the world before and after you have kids. If you travel before kids, not only will it be cheaper but you will have the freedom to explore and party without having to worry about having kids to take care of. Once you have kids, it might be hard to find a babysitter in order for you to go out and party. The added responsibility is definitely a life changer.

Find The Right Person. As you get older you will develop into a different individual. You will gain more values in life and you will outgrow some people. It is best to wait until you develop into the person you will become and wait to meet a woman who has developed as well. Give yourself time to develop, see the world and meet the right person before you have kids. No regrets.

Finances. Do you have enough money to support yourself? Can you pay your own bills? Can you buy your own clothes and food? After you finish school, develop a career, travel a bit, find the right person and marry her, you will be able to sit down and financially say you are ready to have a child. Kids cost money and require time. Build your bank account, buy a house, and get yourself financially set for a child before you have one.

By financially, I mean make sure you can afford a child and everything that comes with having one— clothes, food, Pampers, shelter, daycare, and schooling.

I want you to talk with your parents or guardians and get their input on kids as well. <u>Set yourself up for success!</u> As I said earlier, it was hard for me at 25 working, paying bills and going to school, so I could only imagine how it would be doing it with a child to take care of.

Short Story

When I was younger, I remember seeing my Aunt Sherry with her big house, three kids and her husband (Uncle Joe). He had a great job and she was at home taking care of the family. I asked my mother one day how they became so successful and she said my aunt had been with him for a long time and they worked together as a team. She supported him all the time he was in school and stood by him. I was like, *Wow!*

That helped define for me how to become successful. I had to find a woman who would stand by me while I finished school and got all the money and believe in me just like my aunt believed in my uncle. They were happily married and successful, and back in those days it was even tougher for them because she was black and he was white.

I believe that being around them my visions of success became colorless and it was defined as something that could happen over time through a great partnership and never giving up.

<u>NOTES</u>

Chapter 3 Review

Fill in the Blank. Habits_____!

Name one way that you can stay out of trouble.

You should wait to have kids until you are?

Name 5 reasons why you shouldn't have kids at an early age.

1. _____

2. _____

3. _____

4. _____

5. _____

CHAPTER 4

All About Respect

GAINING RESPECT

Respect is hard to gain and easy to lose. Once you master how to gain respect you will be closer to becoming successful. You gain respect in several different ways:

- Work hard

- Show respect to others

- Show persistence

- Walk the walk

In order to gain respect in life, you have to be a serious person who shows leadership qualities. People respect those who want things out of life, work hard, possess knowledge, and those who can have a conversation about living their dreams. No one respects people who joke around all day, sit around doing nothing and tell lies. Even though the truth sometimes hurts, you will always be respected for telling the truth. Distance yourself from situations that may lead to you throw others under the bus.

I'm not saying you can't joke around sometimes, but first make sure you have everything in order to go along with those jokes.

Work hard. Beat people at their own game! If you are at work and your boss wants you to work hard, work harder. You gain more respect by exceeding people's expectations!

Show respect to others. Be genuine but stand up for what you believe in and be smart enough to get down and dirty for your respect. Everyone deserves to be respected. Try to avoid confrontation by walking away from hostile and disrespectful people and environments that might escalate into unnecessary actions.

Show persistence. Whether you know it or not everyone around you is watching your work ethic and how you carry yourself. Are you a person who quits easily or are you a fighter? Do you get the job done and go for more? Why do you want to be successful? Use your reason as motivation to never give up and you will gain a lot of respect especially by keeping a positive attitude.

Walk the walk. This means "practice what you preach" at all times. If you say something is wrong then don't get caught doing what you said is wrong. Do what you say and say what you mean! Keep your promises and if you know you might not be able to keep them, don't make a promise. Make every effort to make things happen as planned. You have to be the ultimate man—not too cocky but confident ... humble but not a pushover ... loving but stern! Live every day one day at a time. Plan for tomorrow but focus on the daily tasks at hand.

RESPECT WOMEN

As a young man, you are developing into a leader. In this journey you will come across many different types of women as you get older and wiser.

There are a few key points that you have to focus on to be successful around women. Here are some things to consider:

+ Self-Control

+ Values/Be Yourself

+ Relationships

Self-Control. You must have self-control when dealing with women. Women don't like men who drool over them like dogs. Women like confident men who can control themselves in many different situations. If you lack self-control your behavior could potentially come off in a negative fashion.

As you become successful in life, you will face many temptations. Learn to develop your self-control in order to stay focused. Here are a few pointers to help you with self-control: (1) Breathe, (2) Relax, (3) Refocus and (4) Leave.

Core Values. When getting to know women, you should start by paying attention to their values. Values are what they believe in. It is important to pay close attention to the women you are around and be able to understand their value system. Not only is this system important for choosing women, but it is important for friends and family as well. Knowing what a person's values are will show you whether you can relate to them or not.

Here are a few great values to look for in women: Loyal, fun, loving, respectful, passionate, educated and positive.

Women look for similar values in men but most importantly they look for:

Dependability, honesty, motivation, inspiration, respect, courage and love.

There are certain aspects that women care about more, so remember to take the time to get to know the women around you and analyze yourself as well. Go over their values and see whose values match yours the most.

Be Yourself. Who Are You? Looking back at some of the values above, start to ask yourself questions that can show who you are. Are you funny or not? Don't Lie! After you determine your own personal values write down 5 below.

Personal Value List:

1.

2.

3.

4.

5.

Hint #1

Look out for women who only want to be around you because of what you have instead of who you are. They are not worth your time.

Hint #2

Never use your charm and abilities for selfish pleasures. Stay positive! Find a woman who you could see yourself building something with such as a family and a career. You must think about whether she is mentally strong enough to be your wife!

Hint #3

Women love talking about the future, especially with an ambitious young man with dreams.

Relationships. As you get older you will start looking for relationships with young girls. How do you know if she is worthy?

- Pay attention.
- Feel the vibe.
- Never lie to yourself.

When other guys try to talk to her, watch how she handles herself. It is not your job to say anything unless he disrespects her after she turns him down. Try to let her handle herself; that way you don't have to get into any serious altercations because you are becoming a man and we all know you want to protect her! However, if she giggles and flirts then you know she's not ready for you. She has to be firm and serious about her bond between the two of you.

Equality is important, she should do for you just as you do for her because this is a relationship. **Example** - You buy her a birthday gift and she should buy you a birthday gift as well. Sometimes she may want to switch things up and take you out— and that's ok. You both should give and receive in order to feel appreciated.

Communication is the biggest thing when it comes to developing a relationship with a woman. You both have to communicate about everything— even things that aren't comfortable to talk about. You will feel more comfortable once things are out in the open. Your business is your business. Keep your relationship information between you and your partner because there are people who may just want to steal one of you or break you up.

Becoming the kind of man who communicates has its advantages because, even though you are in control, you don't have to brag and boast because your lady already knows who you are. She knows you are her young, smart, hardworking, talented man and she does not want to lose you. So relax because if she's a smart woman she won't mess things up. If you chose the right woman you will feel the same way. This way, you both will appreciate the <u>value</u> of each other.

RESPECT ALL PEOPLE

Based on my own life learned statics...

- Being negative and disrespectful cuts off 50% of your chances to succeed
- Being racist cuts off another 25%

It is best that you love all, work hard, and stay

positive in order to be a force in this society! True leaders understand that we live in a systematic world and there is a certain cycle of good and evil no matter what race you are. If you are black or white, rich or poor, you have an opportunity to be the best you can be throughout your lifetime.

Depending on where you start, you might have to work harder than others. While you are working hard and others are relaxing, remember that you are gaining on them in this race to become successful.

Short Story

The moment I decided I wanted to make a way for my family and leave Chicago I started to realize that I would have to work harder than everyone and stay positive in order to become successful. I had already seen what negativity looked like in my past, plus I knew being lazy would get me nowhere fast.

I arrived in Louisiana and I was in debt like crazy, with a $380 car note that was due and only $200 dollars in my pocket. I was so far behind in debt that I couldn't sleep. I filled out every application online, called every hotel and walked into different places handing out my resume. I was hungry and dedicated.

There were bad environments in Louisiana, just like Chicago, but since nobody knew me I was able to stay to myself and work on building back up. I didn't make friends with everyone, but I was a good person who treated everyone with respect. I was focused on getting my money right so that I could make some major moves in my future.

I had to shift gears and learn to communicate on another level, you see I understood the street level of thinking and blending in but I had to learn the corporate way of blending in. I had to learn how to communicate on a business level with older people who I would come in contact with on a daily basis.

I had a great chef named Jodice who groomed me into a kitchen leader. She taught me it was ok to think bigger and that I wasn't alone. I would sit in her office and tell her stories about my future plans and she encouraged me to be better every day. She gave me my first sous chef promotion at the age of 21, and I was excited but devastated at the same time. This was a tough position as I was becoming the boss of coworkers who were not only my friends but were twice my age. However, nobody went against me since they all respected my work ethic.

I learned that when you lead by example and you speak to everyone around positively, people are more receptive. I also learned that, if you come off negatively you will be eaten alive. I saw some co-workers chew a hole in my executive sous chef when she tried to come at them wrong.

When you respect everyone they will respect you back. Becoming a man of respect starts at the beginning when you first meet an individual and continues throughout your time knowing that person. You have to stay on point at all times. Respect is hard to gain and easy to lose.

– Diamond McNulty

NOTES

CHAPTER 4 REVIEW

Fill in the blank. Respect is hard to gain and

_____.

Name (3) ways in which you gain respect.

Name (2) things you need to be/have in order to be successful around women.

You can tell a lot about a woman by her core

_____.

Being negative and disrespectful cuts off _____% of your chances to succeed.

Being racist cuts off_____% of your chances to succeed.

CHAPTER 5

Fundamentals To Know & Practice

READING

Have you ever heard the saying that if you want to hide something from someone you should put it in a book? Well, the saying is true! Personally, I was a math wizard in school but I really had trouble in my reading classes. I never read books outside of the required schoolbooks and I really didn't care until the age of 24.

It wasn't until I had questions about how to run a music company I was in the process of building that I decided to purchase a book instead of going to school for it. Reading changed my life. Reading to learn became a hobby and I finally realized I could teach myself.

That was the best day of my life because from that day on I found my mind opening up and I felt as if all my questions were being answered. I decided to buy more books and before I knew it I had 10, then 20. Now I have so many books that I've lost count— but for me they are all about my interest in business, mostly things to elevate my knowledge.

Reading and buying books on your own can save you a lot of time and money. It also allows you to meet great people, share or exchange books and gain personal information that the average person may not know or utilize.

It is critical to remember that knowledge is the key that will open doors! We live in a world that swallows the weak. One negative court case and you're cursed for life depending on your environment. The only way to beat the odds is to stay out of trouble, educate yourself and create your own worth. If you happen to get in trouble and it leads to you being convicted of a crime, from then on it will be a challenge to get a good job.

Therefore, having knowledge will allow you to start your own business if necessary and, if you think like me, who really wants to work for someone else his or her whole life anyway?

SELF-MOTIVATION AND PERSISTENCE

Self-motivation is the force that drives you to action.

Persistence is continuing to do a task in spite of how difficult it is or the opposition you face.

Self-motivation and persistence are things you must have on your journey to success because not everyone will support you or tell you that you are doing a good job. With that said, don't dwell on the thoughts of others or your past failures.

Reflecting on the past is ok but it is better to focus on today in order to better your tomorrow! If you got bad grades last quarter, don't dwell on them. Start studying so you can get better grades next time.

Challenge yourself. I know I am cramming a lot of important information in your head and you are probably filled with the excitement to read more. I honestly want you to open your mind and take everything I'm saying into account so that it sticks with you for the rest of your life. Keep referring to this book so you can become successful and stay successful.

FAITH AND MOTIVATION

Faith plays a big part in your road to becoming successful. Success is based on how your mind processes the events in your life. Think… Your brain is a tool so use it to its full potential. When you are stuck in certain situations, think! The situation is not permanent, it is temporary and it will be over soon.

You will value every lesson you get from going through it. What I am saying here is that the more mistakes you make the greater your chances are of becoming successful. Typically it's best to learn from other people's mistakes, which is why I stress listening to older individuals who can give you insight to save you from going through the same things they did.

Believe that all things are possible. Stick to your beliefs with the ultimate sacrifice to yourself that you can do anything. I remember, when I was at my lowest point in life in 2008, instead of letting negativity get the best of me, I used that lowest point as my motivation.

At that moment, since I was at the bottom of the bottom, the only place for me to go was to the top. I sat in my car and laughed because it was funny. I was learning so many lessons at that moment, from who was really by my side to what got me to that point to thinking this would never happen again.

In order to truly become successful, you have to overcome many obstacles—this will make you a stronger individual. This world is not for the weak, but there are benefits for those people who go through the darkness to see the sunny days—trust me; they are worth every moment. Use your family as support and your obstacles as motivation to never stop. Stay focused on the target. A lot of people won't believe in your dreams like you believe, but that's the defining moment of your faith—something that you can't see or grasp but you still choose to believe.

Short Story

Three months before I left Chicago, I was sleeping in my car after my family had split up. I decided to move into my grandmother's five-bedroom house on the South Side of Chicago to bounce back. My uncle immediately kicked me out of my grandmother's house and told me I couldn't stay there. There was only one other person living there at the time; I was hurt beyond belief that he would rather push me to the street instead of letting me live there.

I remember sitting in my car laughing because that was the lowest point I had ever been in my life. I was so faith driven that I asked God to show me everything I needed to see at that moment.

At that moment I learned who were truly my friends, who had my back, and I said I would never get that low ever again. I slept at my girlfriend's house for a few days but her mother didn't really want me there and I respected that. I called my mother's ex-boyfriend (my father figure) who had been in my life since I was two years old and he told me to bring everything I had to his house and I could sleep on his couch.

That meant a lot to me, especially since my mother at that time didn't know I was out on the streets. I could have called my mother and slept on her couch, but she had a one-bedroom apartment and I didn't want to run to her, so I decided to stand strong on my own.

Skipping forward to when I moved to Atlanta from Louisiana, I ran out of money and I called my mother who had just found out that I was homeless before from my ex-girlfriend in Chicago and she was heartbroken. I told her about my situation with my rent and she cleared her savings account to pay it. I was so upset because I was almost homeless again and I felt like a failure. Here I was still taking risk after risk, but deep down inside me I knew I was becoming a success story. After she paid my rent I got a call from a job one week later and started working at a hotel in Atlanta.

If I had given up I probably would have run back home and never fulfilled my destiny. When times get hard, it's easy to give up and it's hard to hold on. After that moment I made it a habit to do everything that was hard in life as a challenge to myself, to see if I could overcome it.

Sometimes you will fall, but you have to dust yourself off and keep going. You will have family members that will hurt you but you have to keep going. Every time I hit rock bottom I told myself I would be the richest man in America and I kept pushing towards my goal. - Diamond McNulty

<u>NOTES</u>

CHAPTER 5 REVIEW

Finish the quote: "If you want to hide something

from someone put it in _____."

"Knowledge is the _____ that will open

doors."

"Reading books can save you_____ and

_____."

Define Self- Motivation.

Define Persistence.

Define Faith.

CHAPTER 6

Start The Journey To Success

DEVELOP LEADERSHIP

When I was 6 years old, I asked my mother if I could go outside to play with the other kids. She responded, "Sure, just don't go to the basketball court across the street because it's very dangerous over there." As a child I didn't understand that my neighborhood was bad and that she was telling me to stay away from the court for my own good. As I went outside, a few of the other kids asked me to go to the basketball court and I went, despite what my mother had just told me.

As I walked inside the house that night she struck me with a firm blow and told me, " BE A LEADER not a follower!" That was the first and last time my mother ever hit me with her bare hands, so it really stood out to me and I knew she was serious—so serious that I can still hear her voice today in every decision I make in life.

Are you a leader or a follower?

A leader is someone who people look up to

A leader is someone who takes responsibility

A leader is someone who creates a vision

A leader is someone who can communicate clearly

A leader is someone who encourages

A leader is confident and inspirational

A leader is dedicated and creative

A leader has a positive attitude

Leaders Lead

To practice good leadership skills, start at home with your family. Whether you are the oldest child or the youngest in the family, it is your duty to help lead the family. Your siblings should look to you for protection and see that you can deliver. With your focus and positive attitude, in no time it will be hard for others not to want to be around you.

Be the one influencing others down the right path instead of letting them influence you to go down the wrong path. <u>Be a leader!</u> Remember, a follower travels behind someone to imitate his or her movements or ideas.

Again, Stay out of Trouble

How can you stay out of trouble? Choose your friends wisely and don't ditch classes.

We've covered the types of friends you should have in your circle but we didn't go over the types of friends you should not have in your circle. Some young men and women around you are into negative things that you should not be involved with.

Peer pressure (influence from others) is big with young women who do not know how to say **NO**. You have a strong mind, right? So you should not have a problem saying **NO** to the pressure of drugs, alcohol or any other reckless activity. Remember, you are in control of what you do. No one can ever make you do anything you don't want to do.

You Are Smart - Make Smart Decisions!

Be a leader not a follower!

EDUCATION & FINANCIAL LITERACY

Financial literacy is the ability to understand how

money works in the world.

Money is to make more money!

Take a moment to look at the chart and picture below:

Education Level	Potential Status	Potential Lifestyle	Potential Influence	Potential Earnings of Money (Yearly)
Entrepreneur	Outer Space	Unlimited	High	Unlimited
Grad School	Moon	High	High	100,000+
College	Sky	Med-High	Med-High	60,000+
High School	Tree	Medium	Medium	+/_ 40,000
Grammar School	Ground	Minimum	Minimum	+/_ 25,000

The picture above describes the levels in life as they pertain to the different levels of education. The higher the level you reach the more money you can acquire. The biggest difference in this picture is that an entrepreneur stands at the top of everything.

Have you ever heard the saying, "The greater the risk the greater the reward"? To become an entrepreneur you can acquire any level of education, but you standout by taking the risk of starting your own business. Some entrepreneurs fail and some succeed. But if you don't take the risk you will never achieve the rewards that go with it.

Traditional education is very important in developing your personal growth, but if you want to become an entrepreneur you will have to work twice as hard and become a leader in business.

College does not guarantee success or guarantee that you will make a lot of money, but there are special benefits that come with higher education. I will teach you skills that you can use in life to become successful. Don't be too hard on yourself if you get a B instead of an A on a test. Challenge yourself and do better next time. Use your shortcomings as motivation to do better. Just continue to be your best at everything you do. Don't let anyone try to make you believe that you cannot achieve something—because anything is possible. Learn how to tell yourself that you did a good job because it builds strength.

"Do your best and forget the rest." – Tony Horton

LEARN TO NETWORK

As you start to travel, you will learn a lot about people, their lifestyles and their culture. After meeting someone you should be able to tell right away if they are someone who can help you or hinder you through the way they communicate.

If they are goal-oriented and business-minded, you should invite them into your circle and carefully get to know them better. If they are not positive, don't waste time on them because people can distract

you from what's really important in life. Every day
is a great day to show the world how focused you are
and you don't have to be arrogant or big-headed
about it. You've got what it takes to be great—just
continue to be humble but focused and you will go
further than you've ever imagined.

Networking with people is part of the process of
building your empire and plan. When you tell people
your dreams, they might look at you like you're
crazy but remember to <u>be bold,</u> your actions speak
louder than words so continue to show and prove.

You will meet people everywhere you go from
school to work and church, and even in different
parts of the world. The world is one big network and
the more access you have the more beneficial it can
become to you. There is a saying that, "Your

Network defines your Net Worth." This means the people you are surrounded by create your value. Just by knowing who you know you might be able to get discounts on certain things, get into places you never knew existed and be invited into different circles. Take advantage of every opportunity.

Short Story

I failed literature my sophomore year in high school and I had to take it up in night school. I hated it because I lived 1 hr. away, and I had to be at school from 7am until late at night to make up the night school class. I blamed my teacher for being a hater and I was disappointed in myself for letting my mom down.

Even though my mom was disappointed she still motivated me to never give up no matter what, which was very refreshing to me, but I was still mad at my teacher. I was so mad I wanted to egg my teacher's car, but instead I swallowed my anger by being the bigger person and did my time quietly.

While taking my night school class, I obviously had to truly do the work so I could pass to the next grade. I started doing my work 100%, reading every chapter and learning new words that I'd never heard before. This sparked an interest in me. Sometimes failing is not failure! You might have to do things over and over in life until you get them right. The only failure is the person who gives up. I made a promise to myself to always try again!

Your destiny is determined by how many times you try again. There is no giving up! There is no, "I quit!" If you have to cry then cry and get back to work. Success is very painful, which is why only the strong survive it. – Diamond McNulty

NOTES

CHAPTER 6 REVIEW

Name two characteristics of leadership.

To practice good leadership skills, start at

_____.

How do you stay out of trouble?

When dealing with peer pressure, what is it best to say?

Define Financial Literacy.

Money is to make more_____.

Networking with people is part of your

_____ process.

Your _____ determines your net worth.

CHAPTER 7

Easy As 1, 2, 3

THINK BIG

Do you want to be the player on the team or the owner of the team? A lot of kids play sports with hopes of becoming a professional athlete. Since not everyone can make it in professional sports, you need to have a backup plan to fall back on while you are working towards your goals.

Have you ever heard anyone say, "I want to become the owner of a sports team"? Trust me; if you think athletes make a lot of money imagine how much money the owners make in order to pay the players. A lot!

I was a great baseball player in high school. I started as a freshman on the varsity team. From a young age, I knew I had some decisions to make during those nights after a game when my bones hurt and I had bruises all over my body from sliding.

I could only imagine how the football players felt smashing into each other, breaking bones and becoming injured for life. That did not seem like much fun to me, especially when they practice so much that they have little time to focus on school.

Many athletes have no knowledge of how business or money works, which is why, after being picked out of hundreds, they get a lot of money and blow it on meaningless things.

Advice: Don't get rich and go broke!

Financial literacy is very important when becoming successful. What is money? How should you use money? How should you not use money? How do you make the most out of each dollar? If you are paid an allowance as a child, it is very important that you use your money wisely because this is the beginning stage of managing money. Money should be used to make more money! Every time you get some money you should think about how you could use it to make more money.

CREATE AND FOLLOW YOUR GOALS

Goals should be divided into 2 categories:

- Short-Term Goals
- Long-Term Goals

Short-Term Goals are goals that you set from today up to the next 5 years.

Long-Term Goals are goals that you set from the 5th year up to 10 years plus.

First things first, you will need a few things to get started:

- A blank notebook and a pencil (so you are able to erase and make changes if needed)
- Write down NOW at the top of the page (your POINT A)
- Write down where you want to be at the bottom of the page (your POINT B)
- Then, depending on where you are in life, write down everything you need to get you from Point A to Point B (example - money, computers, knowledge (school), people you need to meet, etc.) in the specific order of attainment

- Write down an estimate of how long it will take you to get through each step, whether you need to save some money, if you need to pick up a second job or join a networking organization. Although it might take a couple years for you to go to school and save money, <u>stick to the plan</u>! If you have a team of people and they all quit on you, <u>stick to the plan</u>!

Growth. You might invest a lot of time and money into your dreams and things might not go as planned, but I can assure you that, through all the pain and confusion, you will learn what went wrong and why it went wrong. Don't make the same mistakes twice. Take your time and follow your faith so that you don't become like others and quit. It may take you 2 or 3 times to get it right!

Ask questions of older and trustworthy people; they have great advice.

In order to win, you have to set yourself up for success 100%. Do not buy anything without having at least twice the amount of money in your account. Spend a dollar; save a dollar. Try to stay out of debt. Learn about what you're getting yourself into before you jump head-first into it. Remember:

(Books – Books – Books) Research!

No matter what happens, **never give up!**

STICK TO THE PLAN

Sticking to the plan is critical when it comes to becoming a successful young man. Coming up with your plan is the first step! Throughout your next couple of years, as you work towards your goals, you will encounter obstacles that will distract you from your main focus.

Throughout the pain, suffering, confusion, anxiety, helplessness, depressed days and nights you have to pick yourself up and stick to the plan. **Strength** is something that you have to acquire long before you start this journey.

Have the ability to do for self, live your life as if you're the only one—meaning don't depend on anyone or anything. Asking for help is one thing but depending on someone is another. The more you depend on others the weaker you become. It's always great to have people in your corner who can help you, but you want to have the mindset that those people are not really there ... as if there is no safety net if you fail. Failure is not an option.

Short Story

Ever since I was 6 years old, my baseball team won 2nd place. I came in second place so many times I got numb to losing and I learned how to become a true champion. Many times people who win 1st place early in life feel so accomplished that they don't strive for anything else in life.

My senior year in high school we made it to the championship game one last time. At this point in my life I had already won a cooking scholarship for $24,000 for college and this would be my last game as a baseball player.

We were down by 6 runs in the last inning. I was up to bat with bases loaded, 2 outs, 2 strikes on me and my heart was pumping. My whole team was yelling, "Diamante ... Diamante!"

I took a step back from the plate to breathe! My final thought was, *It's not over until we win.* I hit a shot to right field that was dropped by the right fielder and we rallied to win the championship game. That was one of the greatest moments of my life! At our awards ceremony I was awarded MVP.

No matter how many times you come in second place, your greatest victory is yet to come. Instead of rolling over and giving up I chose to fight and focus because my team needed me to deliver. In the time of desperation your team will need you, your family will need you and your future children will need you to step up to the plate and bring it home. It's always easy for us to put the game in someone else's hands, but when you take control of your life, your future and walk in your purpose, you will become successful. – Diamond McNulty

NOTES

CHAPTER 7 REVIEW

You should always think_____ when planning
your goals.

You should always have a backup_____ to fall
back on when working towards your goals.

Define short-term goals.

Define long-term goals.

No matter what happens on your road to success you
should never_____.

_____is something you have to acquire
long before you start this journey.

CHAPTER 8

Becoming A Success

THE MIND FOR SUCCESS

How do you prepare yourself for pain? The stronger you are the less painful things are mentally and physically, so learn to laugh at it and get back to business. Don't consume yourself with the millions of problems in the world that can take you off your "A" game. You only can do what you can do. Work harder than everyone and push it past the limit.

I worked 3 jobs around the clock 7 days straight for 6 months; I eventually cut it down to two so that I could free up time to complete another goal. I analyzed my plan, took time to think, then moved to another city that was better suited to complete that plan. I went to film school and then, again, got 2 jobs as I built multiple companies. I read business books and attended school on my off days.

Don't let anything stop you. Make it happen.

Work harder than everyone.

Organization plays a big role when you start to get to this level. When I left Chicago, my focus was on getting my family to a better place. My mind said, *I'm going to take over the world and this is how I'm going to do it.* Plan, plan, plan!

When you want something so bad, it's hard to sleep. My motto is NO SLEEP, GOTTA GET IT… I rarely feel tired and after 5 years here we are!

When you are doing things that are outside the box and striving for greatness, the attitude of those around you will shift from looking at you like you're crazy to having crazy respect for you, eventually placing you on a high pedestal.

Remember to keep going and focus... Don't gloat or get big-headed. This is just the beginning. When I first started, I found myself working with people who were lazy and didn't want to put in the work it took to become successful. When this happens, it is best to cut them off and get back to business ... just that simple.

There is no time to waste when you are headed to the top... Let's go! Nothing more to talk about ... you are going to the top. Never limit yourself. Never say you can't do something, just do it.

One thing I have noticed about myself is that I always fit better around older people because we think on the same level. We all believe that life is not a game. My circle was and still is full of skilled individuals who think like me.

If I meet you once, I already know if you are genuine. I pick up on things quickly and, depending on our conversation, the connection will be built or broken instantly. I'm a great chef but I have no problem washing dishes, if that what it takes to get where I am trying to go. You have to start somewhere.

What also keeps me motivated is remembering how much my mother sacrificed for me. It's a goal of mine to become the best I can be, not only because I'm working hard to take over the world but because I'm going to give her the opportunity to relax. She deserves it. Don't be a burden to others, especially your parents just because they will do anything for you. Don't abuse them. Make their lives easier. Not everyone may be a supporter but everyone means something. Have respect for all people.

You will become very successful but along with success comes responsibility—what is the plan after you become successful? How many lives will you change? I have a full-blown plan because all I do is think and plan.

Most people don't use their brain to its full potential. Use Yours! Who cares if someone else was born filthy rich and you were born poor? Who cares that your father wasn't there? Who cares what you didn't have? I'll let you in on a little secret—the world does not care! Your life is in your hands. Once you hit 18 and older, you are responsible for yourself. Take the negative that has been thrown your way and turn it into a positive.

Are you willing to leave everything behind to chase your dream? Are you willing to sleep on the floor and barely eat? We all have to start somewhere. When others are working, I'm working. While others are watching TV, I'm working. When they are sleeping, I'm just coming home, taking a shower, and planning the future while I shower, brushing my teeth and building my team, laying down and planning for tomorrow. Don't stop! Keep going.

If you've been to one party you've been to them all. If you focus now, by the time you're older you will have accomplished your goals and have become a successful young man.

I didn't know how to cook, write music, rap, create logos, create websites, film movies or play chess until I studied those crafts and built those skills. Everyone doubted me except for a handful of people. My mind was made up from the beginning that I had a few talents and I wanted to get better at them all.

If cooking didn't work, I would do film. If film didn't work, I would do music. I worked them all at the same time so that no matter what happened I would be successful. I would cook and create songs while at work, visually planning the videos and creating the website concept all at once in my head.

Many people focus on one thing at a time, but I have a different belief system. When I was 16, my mentor Mr. Muhammad told me never to put all my eggs in one basket. I stuck to that belief and it has gotten me far in life.

Every business-minded individual should learn business and accounting. You have to study hard in order to master your future. Adopt a mind for success. Anything is possible!

THE SECRET TO SUCCESS

The Law of Attraction is the secret to success, meaning surround yourself with things and people that will keep you in line with your goals. Also, you have to speak success into existence! The more you say things and act on them the more likely you will achieve them. People follow people who they can trust because **Great Leaders Lead.**

That secret is already out, but applying that secret is the key to success. Knowing and applying are two different things. Every day I open my eyes with a positive attitude and tell myself, "I'm going to take over the world." I have <u>faith,</u> which means I believe that my dreams and visions will come true, given the hard work and dedication I put towards making them happen. When anyone asked me how I was doing, I would say, "I'm doing great, taking over the world one day at a time." Every day those were my words! And I truly applied that to my life.

In my living room, I have put up a map up of the world so that every time I'm on my computer I can see it.

Whenever I take a trip or travel to a place or even meet someone from another state or country, I mark it on my map! I started asking different people from different countries what kind of businesses they had in their country and what they wanted to really do outside of their current jobs because some people also have dreams that might align with yours. I dream of bettering the world and helping someone else.

I hope you have received all of this information and that you take it to heart. You should have great intentions and now you should feel more equipped to accomplish your goals in life. I wish you much success, love and happiness on Becoming A Successful Young Man.

Short Story

The older I get the more thankful I am. You can gain a lot by being a good person. Two of the most important things that helped me become successful were taking advantage of every program that was available to me to help expand my talents/skills and having great mentors who guided me on my path to success.

At 7 years old, my mother placed me in the Chicago Youth Programs that every Saturday took us on field trips and paired us up with professional mentors who not only tutored us but cared about us. I am very grateful to Dr. Joe DiCara and Dr. Karen Sheehan because that one seed that was planted 20 years ago will change the lives of children around the world. Thank you to the full CYP staff, mentors and Josephine and Bill Johnson.

You see, giving is a domino effect and we all must do our job to pay it forward as well. I am very active when it comes to teaching kids how to live their dreams and when a child becomes successful it is their responsibility to pay it forward as well.

Every summer my mother allowed me to play on the baseball team where I had coaches who took us to meet professional baseball players like Frank Thomas, back when he was the most popular player in Chicago. These same coaches recommended me to take two summer courses with NFTE—National Foundation for Teaching Entrepreneurship—which helped me develop my entrepreneur mindset. I have to thank coaches Kevin Kalinich, Steve Bridges, Kyle, Craig and all the other coaches from the Bakongo Little League Baseball Team. You might all know the movie *Hardball*, which was based off of our team.

Then, as time passed, I met Mr. Muhammad in high school who showed me multiple life principles that enhanced my thinking and expanded my wisdom through reading. It is definitely true when we say that it takes a village to raise a child. Even today I have two more mentors, Reginald Grand Pierre and Stacey Brown, who have helped me master another level of success "family".

Take advantage of every program that is offered to you and look for older mentors who truly want you to succeed and grow. All you have to do is listen, put in the work and have faith. Once again I wish you much success. Stay positive and the world is yours. – Diamond McNulty

Repeat After Me

I can do anything I put my mind to!

I can become anything I want to become!

I will work hard and pursue my dreams!

I will never give up!

I will be successful!

THE SUCCESS PLAN

In this portion of the book we will assist you in starting your journey to becoming a successful young man.

For the full success plan, please purchase the

How To Become A Successful Young Man

workbook at:

www.SuccessfulYoungMan.com

THE VISION BOARD

"Taking Over The World"

As an initial step in developing a success plan, you will need to create a vision board. I want you to go to your nearest store and pick up 1 dry erase board, 1 dry board erase marker, 1 poster board and 1 map of the world. You will also need to collect some old newspaper and magazines.

Next, I want you to answer each question below on the dry erase board and hang it on a wall in your room. With the poster board you can either write on your board the things you want to accomplish or stick pictures of the things you want to accomplish to it and place it somewhere in your room so you can see it every day. Also, place the map of world in a place where you can view it every day as well.

What do you want to be in life?
Doctor, lawyer, political figure, entrepreneur, sports owner, etc.

Name 2 backup plans.

What do you want to accomplish in your lifetime?
Your own company, a house, car, spouse,
recognition

How will you make a difference in society? *Give*
back to the youth? Become a volunteer, mentor,
donate?

Name every material thing you want. Price?

Name every material thing you need to
accomplish your goals. Price?
(Clothes, computer, gadgets, TVs, piano, etc.)

What steps do you need to take to achieve your
goals?

What schools will you attend? College? Graduate
School etc.?

Where are the best places to do internships for
your career?

Name the places you would live to travel to.

List some hobbies you would like to acquire.

Write down the titles of 3 books you would like to
read.

NOTES

CHAPTER 8 REVIEW

The _____ you are the less painful
things are mentally and physically.

You should always have a _____ for when you
become successful.

Surround yourself with _____ that will keep
you in line with your goals.

ABOUT THE AUTHOR

Diamond McNulty was born and raised in the Cabrini Green housing projects on the North Side of Chicago, Illinois. Surrounded by gang violence, drugs and minimal opportunities, McNulty has achieved what many people believe to be "The Impossible". Overcoming various obstacles, he has created a system for success despite the odds he was dealt. It goes to say that in order to gain it all you must lose it all. The one thing that McNulty grasped that many kids don't at a young age is the ability to listen and pay attention.

Leaving Chicago with $200 in his pocket, all McNulty had were a boat load of expenses, student loans and a dream. His journey took hard work, faith, motivation, persistence and patience over the years to overcome what many believe to be the ultimate struggle. By winning various scholarships, teaching cooking classes, and mentoring kids, he has dedicated his life to giving kids the knowledge it takes to become successful.

Through every struggle, McNulty embraced his experience as an opportunity to learn and grow. He surrounded himself with people like himself and learned the difference between gambling and investing. By traveling alone from city to city, he set his goals and executed them one day at a time. He worked 3 jobs around the clock in order to pay for college and start up his first 4 companies. He continues to grow into a prominent individual in society. McNulty is very grateful for every mentor that has entered his life and kept him on the right path along his journey to "Take Over The World".

Diamond McNulty is currently the CEO of McNulty International and corporate executive chef of Taste of Diamond Catering. For more details go to:

www.DiamondMcnulty.com